CLIMATE CHANGE

TECHNOLOGICAL SOLUTIONS

BY JIM OLLHOFF

VISIT US AT
WWW.ABDOPUBLISHING.COM

Published by ABDO Publishing Company, 8000 West 78th Street, Suite 310, Edina, MN 55439. Copyright ©2011 by Abdo Consulting Group, Inc. International copyrights reserved in all countries. No part of this book may be reproduced in any form without written permission from the publisher. ABDO & Daughters™ is a trademark and logo of ABDO Publishing Company.

Printed in the United States of America, North Mankato, Minnesota
052010
092010

 PRINTED ON RECYCLED PAPER

Editor: John Hamilton
Graphic Design: Sue Hamilton
Cover Photos: iStockphoto
Interior Photo: AP-pgs 7, 8, 16, 22, 25, 27 & 28; Getty Images-pgs 5, 19, 24 & 26; iStockphoto-pgs 1, 4, 6, 15, 20 & 23; NASA-pg 12; Photo Researchers-pgs 11, 13 & 29; Thinkstock-pg 32; U.S. Department of Energy-pg 14; Visuals Unlimited-pg 17; White House-pg 21; Windspire Energy-pg 9.

Library of Congress Cataloging-in-Publication Data

Ollhoff, Jim, 1959-
 Technological solutions / Jim Ollhoff.
   p. cm. -- (Climate change)
 Includes index.
 ISBN 978-1-61613-457-0
 1. Climatic changes--Prevention--Technological innovations--Juvenile literature. 2. Climatic changes--Risk management--Juvenile literature. 3. Global warming--Prevention--Technological innovations--Juvenile literature. 4. Global warming--Risk management--Juvenile literature. I. Title.
 QC903.15.O46 2010
 363.738'74--dc22
                    2010005522

CONTENTS

TECHNOLOGICAL SOLUTIONS

Above: A large bulldozer works on a mountain of garbage in a county landfill.

Facing Page: Millions of cars pump carbon dioxide into the atmosphere. Can science help us fix the world's problems?

Most climate scientists agree that the world is getting warmer, and humans are to blame. We burn fossil fuels, we drive cars that pollute, we have too much garbage, we burn forests, and we do many other things that hurt the environment.

Scientists also agree that although the earth is warming, it is still early in the process. Humans may be causing climate change, but humans can still stop it. The longer we wait, the more difficult and expensive it will be. If we wait too long, very advanced technology might be needed to stop global warming.

This book explains several ways to stop global warming. They are technological solutions. They are things we can build, or ways we can act, to slow down or stop the warming process. Some of these ideas require humans to manipulate the earth's climate. This is called geoengineering, or engineering the earth. While these geoengineering ideas haven't been tried yet, they have caught the imagination of many people.

MOVE TO RENEWABLE ENERGY

Above: Carbon dioxide spews out of a car's tailpipe. *Facing Page:* Wind turbines in front of a coal-fueled power plant. In recent years, there has been a move to renewable energy.

When humans burn fossil fuels to make electricity or power vehicles, carbon dioxide is created. The burning of coal, oil, and natural gas is the source of about 33 percent of the carbon in the atmosphere. Any solution to global warming must help us depend less on fossil fuels. Other sources of energy need to be used.

There are many problems with fossil fuels. Burning coal, oil, and natural gas creates heat-trapping greenhouse gasses. Pollution is another problem. Coal is the worst polluter. It releases a lot of toxic chemicals into the environment. Another problem with fossil fuels is that they won't last forever. Coal will probably last two hundred years or more. Oil production, however, could be peaking very soon.

There are two big advantages of fossil fuels. First, they are cheap. Second, the world's industries are already set up to burn coal, oil, and natural gas. Power plants and the electric grid already rely on fossil fuels. Our vehicles burn gasoline, which is made from oil. Gas stations are set up to receive and deliver the gasoline. Almost every part of our society uses fossil fuels in some way. This makes it difficult to stop using them.

Solar and wind energy produce no pollution or greenhouse gasses. They are called renewable energy sources because their power will never run out. The wind will always blow, and the sun will always shine. Switching to renewable energy, and doing so quickly, could halt the ever-increasing amounts of carbon dioxide in the earth's atmosphere.

Today, solar and wind energy are expensive compared to fossil fuels. But prices are expected to drop as more people purchase and use the technology. World governments can also help pay for renewable energy until prices are lower.

Another advantage of renewable energy is that it's possible for small customers to generate their own power.

Below: Solar-powered roof shingles help power this home in Virginia.

For example, homes could have their own small windmill or solar-powered roof shingles. In this way, homes could generate their own power and then sell the extra electricity back to a central electric utility. Some European countries have used this model very successfully.

A vertical wind turbine from Windspire Energy is 30 feet (9 m) tall and 4 feet (1.2 m) wide. This type of mini-wind turbine helps to power homes and small businesses.

A TRILLION MIRRORS

Too much carbon dioxide in the atmosphere causes sunlight to overheat the earth. Is it possible to block some of the sunlight? Scientists have explored this idea. They estimate that using a giant mirror or screen to deflect just one percent of the sunlight would keep the earth's climate stable. The screen could be put in orbit between the sun and the earth, always blocking part of the sun's warming energy. The problem is that it would require a massive screen. It would measure at least 600,000 square miles (1,553,993 sq km). That's almost the size of Alaska.

Other scientists say that if the screen were closer to the sun, it would only need to measure about 41 sq miles (106 sq km). They estimate that the project would take about 100 years to complete. It would require 100 shuttle missions to transport and assemble the screen in space.

Another idea is to use smaller screens, but a lot more of them. Millions of screens, perhaps even trillions, would be needed. Each of these screens would be about the size of a large dinner plate. Scientists have even considered shooting them into orbit with a huge cannon that has a barrel one mile (1.6 km) long.

Facing Page: A giant circular mirror could be designed to shield the earth from the sun in order to stabilize the world's climate.

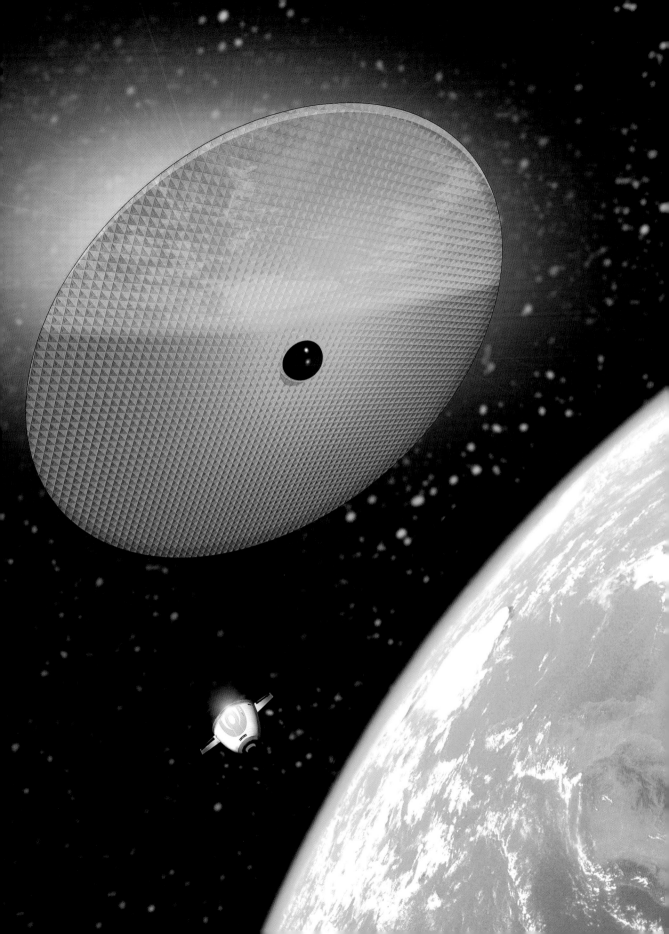

Above: The Space Shuttle *Discovery's* payload bay is opened while docked at the International Space Station. Although today's spacecraft are able to transport huge loads, the technology to get millions of mirrors into space does not yet exist.

There are many problems with the idea of blocking sunlight. The expense would be huge. Making the mirrors would require vast amounts of natural resources. The technology to get the mirrors into space doesn't yet exist. The production and transportation of the mirrors would also produce greenhouse gasses.

Worst of all, deflecting sunlight will not solve the problem of global warming. It will merely deflect a symptom of the problem. Even if we launched a trillion mirrors, as long as we keep using fossil fuels, we'll still be adding carbon dioxide to the atmosphere. That means in 20 years, we would have to put even more mirrors into orbit.

With the money it would take to put a trillion mirrors into orbit, the world could completely convert to renewable energy for almost all of our electricity and transportation needs. This would solve the problem of greenhouse gasses, instead of just covering up a symptom.

A California wind farm produces clean power.

NUCLEAR POWER

Facing Page: A nuclear power plant at night.
Below: A graphic from the United States Department of Energy shows where radioactive fuel is stored.

S ome people believe that we should stop using fossil fuels and switch to nuclear power instead. Nuclear power already provides about 15 percent of the world's electricity needs. Nuclear power produces no carbon dioxide and no greenhouse gasses. Some people have suggested that we could build 5,000 nuclear power plants and shut down all the fossil fuel plants.

The nuclear power industry says that today's nuclear power plants are safer than previous generations of nuclear plants. However, nuclear power is very expensive to produce. Also, many people don't trust the industry's spotty safety record.

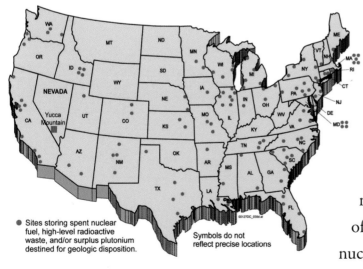

● Sites storing spent nuclear fuel, high-level radioactive waste, and/or surplus plutonium destined for geologic disposition.

Symbols do not reflect precise locations

One of the unanswered questions of nuclear power has to do with radioactive waste. Nuclear power plants have a waste product that is highly toxic. It stays radioactive for thousands of years. If we built 5,000 nuclear power plants, what would we do with all that waste? How would nuclear engineers safely store it? How would they keep radiation from leaking into rivers, or contaminating groundwater?

SEA GATES AND LEVEES

Above: In 2005, Hurricane Katrina damaged several levees in New Orleans, Louisiana. Sandbags were used to stop the terrible flooding.

One of the big problems with global warming is that sea levels are predicted to rise. Many coastal areas will be flooded. One plan is to build massive levees and sea gates to keep rising oceans from flooding populated areas. A levee is a wall that keeps the ocean from flooding onto the land. A sea gate can be opened to let boat traffic in and out of a harbor, but can close when a hurricane approaches. Hurricanes bring giant surges of water that can create massive damage.

Some countries, like the Netherlands, have had very strong levees for decades. Some countries have built sea gates, and many other countries are considering them.

One of the problems, of course, is that levees and sea gates are very expensive. Richer countries could build them. Poorer countries could not. Some low-lying areas without levees, such as Southeast Asia, could be devastated by hurricanes. Millions of people would lose their land and homes.

The biggest problem with this idea is that it doesn't really deal with the problem of climate change. It only deals with the rising ocean levels once climate change has already happened. Some levees will probably have to be built. But the problem of global warming is still early enough that the worst of the effects can be stopped, if we're willing to make big changes.

Above: An earthen levee along the Mississippi River.

BIOCHAR

When grasses or other organic materials are heated slowly without oxygen, a black material resembling charcoal is the result. This is called biochar. It is a black, chunky material made mostly of carbon. It is this ability to hold carbon that excites scientists. Carbon can be pulled out of the air and held in the biochar.

The other exciting thing about biochar is that putting it into the ground makes the soil richer. It holds water, keeps soil nutrients in place, and adds nutrients that make the soil more fertile. Because of farming, much soil all over the world is depleted of nutrients. People like the idea of adding richness to the soil and sequestering, or trapping, carbon at the same time.

Any organic material can be used to make biochar, from woodchips to cow manure. For centuries, tribes in the Amazon rainforest burned organic material in pits covered with dirt. This process produced biochar. The tribes used the biochar to enrich their soil for farming.

The problem with biochar is scale. Could farmers ever produce enough biochar to get a significant amount of carbon out of the atmosphere? It seems unlikely. So, while biochar is a good idea, it probably can't solve the climate crisis by itself.

Above: Although it looks like charcoal, the black chunks are biochar. A poultry farmer churns out biochar from chicken waste and wood chips, turning it into a valuable fertilizing substance that is also environmentally clean.

CARBON SEQUESTERING

Above: Is there a way to clean our air?

If there is too much carbon in the atmosphere, could some of it be taken out of the atmosphere and buried? This process is called carbon sequestering. It is an idea that is now being explored by scientists. Could the carbon from fossil fuel-burning power plants be captured, and then sequestered deep underground? Could it be buried in deep caverns or in the places where oil was once drilled? No one knows for sure, but scientists are experimenting with those ideas.

Some scientists propose building windscrubbers. These machines would have giant panels that filter carbon dioxide out of the air. The carbon would be turned into a liquid and then buried deep underground.

No one knows if carbon sequestering will work. It's possible that the carbon dioxide might leak out and get back into the atmosphere. Could it leak into buildings, where it could be fatal to people? Scientists are trying to answer these very questions.

Carbon Sequestration Options

Above: Is there a way to take excess carbon out of the atmosphere? Scientists are exploring the process of doing just that. The process is called carbon sequestration. The idea is to remove excess carbon from the atmosphere and "sequester," or store, it underground.

SEED THE CLOUDS

High, white clouds reflect sunlight. These reflected rays don't reach the earth, and can't create heat. Is there a way to make more of these kind of clouds to reflect the sun's heat and light? Many scientists think it can be done with a process called cloud seeding. Dropping the right kind of chemicals from high-flying airplanes might increase cloud cover.

Another possibility is to spray seawater high up into the air. This fine mist would make water droplets whiter, which would make them more reflective. The thicker cloud cover would reflect more sunlight back into space. Some scientists estimate that a fleet of 1,500 water-spraying ships could increase the cloud cover.

Below: A small airplane with a cloud-seeding device mounted on the wing.

Above: Scientists wonder if there is a way to seed the clouds to make them reflect more of the sun's heat and light. What people don't know is how a thicker cloud cover could affect plants, animals, and the earth itself.

However, these ideas have never been tried. Chemicals used in cloud seeding could be harmful to humans or other living things. Salt particles in seawater spray might create a drought instead of more clouds. And what other effects would these activities cause? Would they disrupt bird life? Would it be harder for plants to grow without as much sunlight? Scientists don't yet know how cloud seeding would affect other parts of our connected world.

SEED THE OCEANS

The earth's oceans are giant natural resources that are already getting rid of carbon. Scientists call the oceans carbon sinks, places that absorb and store carbon. The oceans are carbon sinks mainly because of plankton, which includes algae, bacteria, plants, and animals that float or drift with the ocean water. Plankton gobbles up carbon dioxide, then converts it into oxygen. Could scientists increase the amount of plankton in the oceans so that more carbon dioxide is absorbed?

Simply adding iron dust to the oceans would cause large-scale plankton growth, called a plankton bloom. This is because plankton feeds on the iron particles. The problem is that the web of relationships in the oceans is not well understood. In other words, if scientists create a plankton bloom, could something unexpected happen also?

Right: Plankton include algae, bacteria, plants, and animals that float or drift with the ocean water. Plankton absorbs carbon dioxide, then converts it into oxygen.

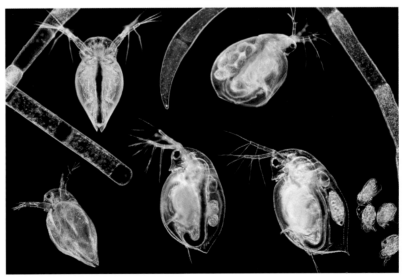

Above: An outbreak of blue-green algae is seen along the coast of eastern China. As scientists consider creating additional plankton blooms in the ocean to absorb carbon dioxide, they must consider the effects these blooms will have on the environment as a whole.

Would plankton gorge itself on all the other nutrients in the water, making it impossible for other sea creatures to live in the area? What happens when the plankton dies? Some scientists think that dead plankton will sink to the bottom of the ocean. But what if it floats to the top, releasing even more carbon dioxide and methane?

Iron makes seawater more acidic. Would that make it difficult for shellfish to create shells? Would the seawater dissolve their shells?

Much more research needs to be done before scientists know for sure whether creating plankton blooms would help reduce carbon dioxide, or make the problem worse.

OTHER IDEAS

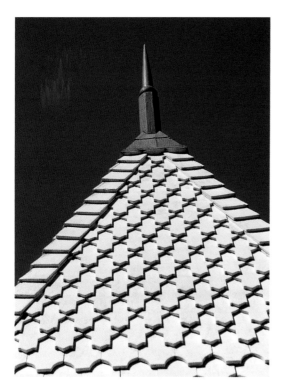

Above: Some think that white roof tiles on homes would help reflect sunlight back into space.

There are many other ideas about how to stop climate change. Some ideas are worth considering. No idea is perfect, some are silly, and some border on being dangerous.

Some scientists say we should insulate glaciers by covering them with reflective tarps. Others say we should cover deserts with reflective tarps, bouncing sunlight back into space. Some scientists say we should paint every rooftop in the world white.

Others scientists say we should inject sulfur high into the atmosphere. This would reflect more sunlight, although the other effects of using sulfur are unknown.

Making cars that run on fuel cells, instead of gasoline, might be one solution. Fuel cells burn cleanly, and the only waste product is clean water. Others say fuel cells could power homes and buildings as well. The problem is that the technology isn't finished yet. No one knows if fuel cells will work on a large scale.

Could carbon be stored in limestone? Could buildings full of algae pull carbon from the air? There are many ideas out there, even more are needed.

Above: In 2007, Honda introduced the FCX Clarity, a car that uses no gasoline. Instead, hydrogen and oxygen are converted by fuel cells into electricity. The vehicle runs totally on this electricity. The Clarity emits no greenhouse gasses, only clean water vapor.

IS IT ALREADY TOO LATE?

Most climate scientists say that there is still time before global warming gets too bad. They say that if we act quickly and strongly, we won't see the worst effects of climate change. They say we need to switch to wind and solar energy, change our transportation systems, adopt more sustainable agricultural practices, and reduce, reuse, and recycle. Most scientists say we still have time to evade the worst damage.

However, there are a small but growing number of scientists who say that stopping production of carbon dioxide will not be enough. These scientists take a more extreme view, and say that it is too late to do simple things to stop global warming. We must consider radical ideas, too. For those scientists, geoengineering is a solution worth considering.

Left: Plastic bottles are stacked at a recycling station. Today, only 2 out of 10 plastic bottles are recycled. Billions more end up in landfills.

Above: Most climate scientists say there is still time to reduce or reverse the effects of climate change. We need to try many ideas. This illustration shows some technological solutions being considered. Two types of space mirrors are shown reflecting sunlight. A hot-air balloon, a plane, or even a specially-designed ship on the ocean may be used for cloud-seeding, which thickens the earth's clouds and blocks some of the sun's light. Solar reflectors may be placed on land or in the seas. Marine life, such as kelp and plankton, may be grown to absorb and store carbon. However, scientists are still investigating how difficult, or dangerous, it is to control the earth's climate.

GLOSSARY

CARBON DIOXIDE

Normally a gas, carbon dioxide is a chemical compound made of two oxygen atoms and one carbon atom. Its chemical symbol is CO_2. It is created by burning fossil fuels. It is the leading cause of the greenhouse effect and global warming.

CARBON SEQUESTERING

Taking carbon from the air and burying it or making it otherwise inert.

CLIMATE CHANGE

The climate of the earth, which consists of the weather all over the world for decades or centuries, and how it is changing.

FOSSIL FUEL

Fuels that are created from the remains of ancient plants and animals that were buried and then subjected to millions of years of heat, pressure, and bacteria. Oil and coal are the most common fossil fuels burned to create electricity. Natural gas is also a fossil fuel. Burning fossil fuels releases carbon dioxide into the atmosphere, contributing to global warming.

GEOENGINEERING

Engineering the earth to counteract climate change.

GLACIER

An immense sheet of ice that moves over land, growing and shrinking as the climate changes. Glaciers carve and shape the land beneath them. Glaciers today are found in the polar regions, and in mountainous areas. They hold vast reserves of fresh water.

GREENHOUSE EFFECT

Just as heat is trapped in a greenhouse by glass, certain gasses in the atmosphere trap the sun's heat and warm the earth. The surface of the earth absorbs some solar radiation, and reflects some. The reflected rays either pass back into space, or are absorbed and reflected back by gasses in the earth's atmosphere. Carbon dioxide is a major greenhouse gas that is produced by burning fossil fuels. When too much solar radiation is absorbed, the earth warms up, which alters climates around the world.

GREENHOUSE GAS

Any gas that is good at absorbing and retaining the sun's heat. Carbon dioxide, which is released into the atmosphere by the burning of fossil fuels, is a greenhouse gas. Greenhouse gasses contribute to a gradual warming of the earth, which is called the greenhouse effect.

METHANE

A gas that is created when organic materials decay.

PLANKTON

Algae, plants, bacteria, and animals that float in the ocean.

PLANKTON BLOOM

When a colony of plankton suddenly becomes much larger. A bloom will cause the surrounding surface water to turn a green or brown color.

INDEX